Strings Connected

Workbook Level Two

Second Edition

Nathan F. P. Fernandes

2nd ed. ISBN: 978-0-9865518-8-8, published 2023

1st ed. ISBN: 978-0-9865518-4-0, published 2003

Published by

stringsconnected.ca

Introduction

Welcome to *Strings Connected Workbook Level Two*, a student workbook that can be used independently or with a teacher.

Designed for experienced students, this workbook continues lessons from *Strings Connected Workbook Level One* and introduces advanced lessons. You will continue to develop your musicianship skills while reading and performing from a more challenging repertoire of songs in various styles of music. You will also be introduced to lifting (figuring out by ear) simple melodies and chord progressions.

Self-discipline is a great quality to have whether you're learning on your own or with a teacher because much of your time practicing is spent alone—without a teacher present. However, being disciplined is not the only quality needed to ensure your best possible development. It's also important that you know how to practice efficiently and progress continuously. Realizing the purpose of each lesson throughout this workbook will help you monitor your own progress. Maintaining a steady flow of small, reachable goals is good for your overall progress and accomplishments.

Remember to relax, take your time, and have fun while learning!

You can download the accompaniment MP3 collection from Strings Connected: stringsconnected.ca

Contents

Lesson One 1

    Accidentals and Key Signatures 2

        Chromatic Notes 3

        Intervals 3

    The G Major Scale 3

    Playing in the Key of G Major 4

        The D7 Chord 5

Lesson Two 6

    4th String or Open D 7

    The D Major and F Major Scales 8

    Reading on the Top 4 Strings 9

Lesson Three 11

    5th String or Open A 12

    The C Major and B^b Major Scales 13

    Reading on the Top 5 Strings 14

Lesson Four 16

    6th String or Open E 17

    Reading and Playing Full Chords 19

Lesson Five 21

    Primary Chords 22

Lesson Six 24

    Name These Melodies 25

Figure Out the Missing Notes 27

Lesson Seven 29

Classical Music 30

Country Music 31

Hammer-ons and Pull-offs 31

Jazz Music 32

Turnaround Progressions 32

Chord Melodies 32

Blues Music 33

Double-stop Riffs 33

Lesson Eight 34

Overview 35

Certificate of Completion 36

Lesson One

Accidentals and Key Signatures

Accidentals

There are twelve different pitches from one octave to the next octave (e.g., from C to the next C). We only use the first seven letters of the alphabet to name all twelve of these pitches. We do this by using accidentals, which raise and lower the pitch of a note without changing the letter-name.

Sharp	♯	Raises the pitch by one semitone (up one fret)
Flat	♭	Lowers the pitch by one semitone (down one fret)
Natural	♮	Restores a note to its natural pitch (no sharps or flats)

Key Signatures

A notation of one or more sharps or flats, placed at the beginning of each staff, is called a key signature. This key signature predefines the accidentals used throughout the song; all octaves are affected. By reading the key signature, you can determine the key of a song. A key signature will have either sharps or flats, not both, and there is a specific order in which these sharps or flats appear.

Accidentals are sometimes used within a song to cancel any predefined notes in the key signature. This is considered non-diatonic (playing outside the key). In such cases, the change is temporary, until the completion of that measure, and only that octave is changed.

If you understand this correctly, the following example should make sense.

The natural notes, in a key signature, are equally as important as the sharp or flat notes. Playing outside the key can also mean changing a predefined natural note to a sharp note or flat note.

Chromatic Notes

Chromatic notes involve the use of accidentals to include all twelve notes in music. For example, there's a note between F and G, and this note can be called either F sharp or G flat. It's one fret higher than F; it's also one fret lower than G. Enharmonic notes are exactly the same in pitch but written differently on the staff.

Intervals

An interval is the distance between two pitches. This distance can be measured by counting the number of whole tones or semitones (also called whole steps or half-steps) between the two notes. A semitone is the shortest interval, which is why semitones are only one fret apart. Whole tones (or just "tones") are two frets apart. F to F sharp is an example of a semitone, and F to G is an example of a tone.

The G Major Scale

A major scale is a series of notes that follows a specific pattern of tones and semitones. This pattern is predefined by the key signature. Starting from the keynote (the note that gives the key its name), play all notes in order, up to its octave. These eight notes, from the keynote to its octave, form a major scale. You might recognize this sound as "Do, Re, Mi, Fa, Sol, La. Ti, Do" (solfege). Letter-names are never skipped or repeated, which is never a problem because there are only seven different notes; the eighth note of the scale is the octave. Notice that "Do" is repeated as the eighth note in solfege.

The major scale pattern of tones (T) and semitones (ST) is T – T – ST – T – T – T – ST. All major scales conform to this pattern of tones and semitones. When starting this pattern from the note G, we need to change F to F sharp, giving us a tone followed by a semitone: E, F sharp, G. Therefore, the key of G major has one sharp in the key signature, which is F sharp. You can play F sharp on the first string at the second fret with your second finger.

G Major Scale

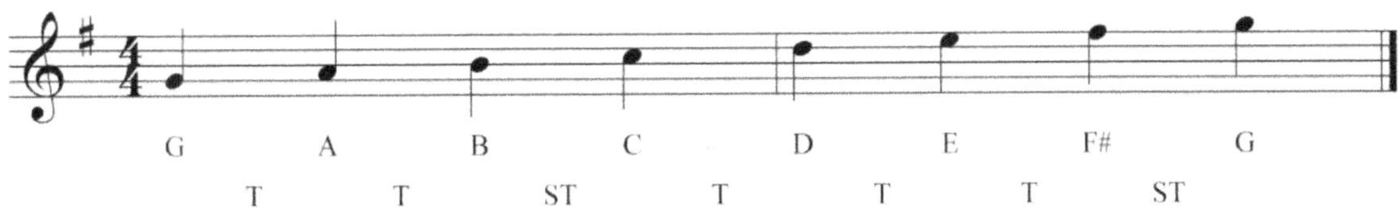

Exercise 1

Practicing this scale both ascending (going up) and descending (going down). You can test how well you know the names of the notes on the fretboard by saying the names as you play the notes descending. Remember to always say "sharp," or "flat," when needed.

Playing in the Key of G Major

Exercise 1

Exercise 2

Exercise 3

Can Can

Keys, chords, and scales can be major or minor. When naming them, saying "major" after the keynote is optional. The key of G, for example, is assumed to be the key of G major. You must, however, say "minor" when naming a minor key or minor chord or minor scale. This is similar to the use of "plus" and "minus" when referring to the temperature.

The D7 Chord

When spelling this chord, you have A, C, and F sharp, which are all fretted notes. Play A with your second finger, C with your first finger, and F sharp with your third finger.

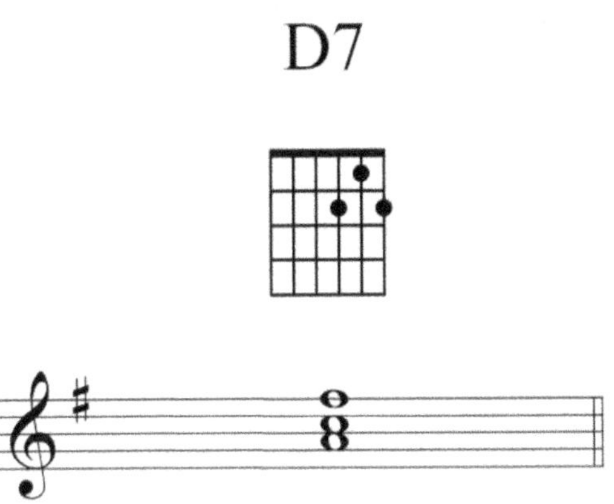

How Much Is That Doggie In The Window?

When playing F sharp, use your second finger for the melody and your third finger for the D7 chord. Sometimes only the chord names are given above the melody. This is enough to tell you which chords are used and when the changes occur. You are expected to ad-lib (improvise) the way the chords are played.

Lesson Two

4th String or Open D

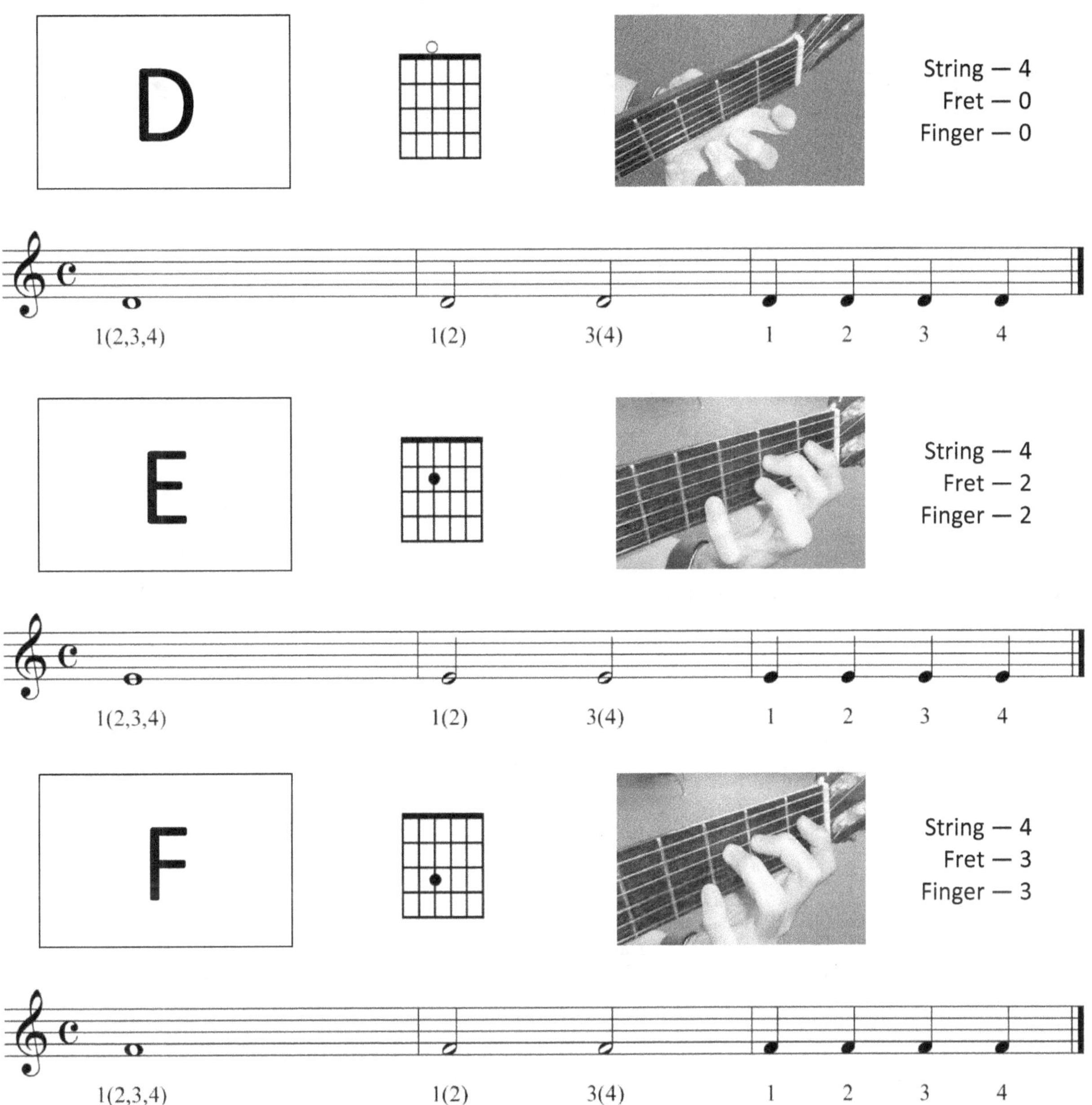

Remember to keep your left-hand fingers spread out so that each finger is close to its own fret.

The D Major and F Major Scales

D Major Scale

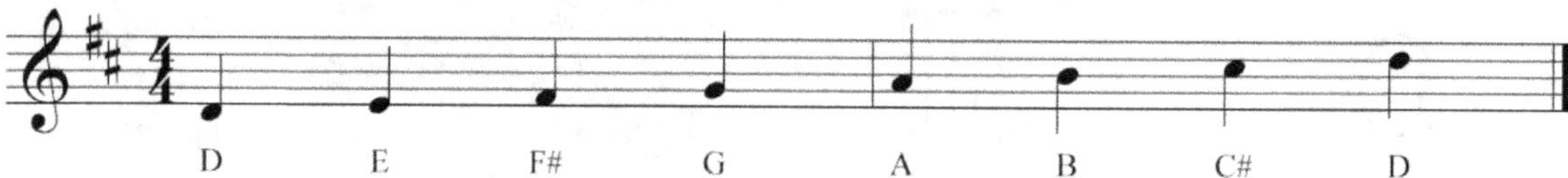

You can play F sharp on the fourth string at the fourth fret with your fourth finger. You can play C sharp on the second string at the second fret with your second finger.

F Major Scale

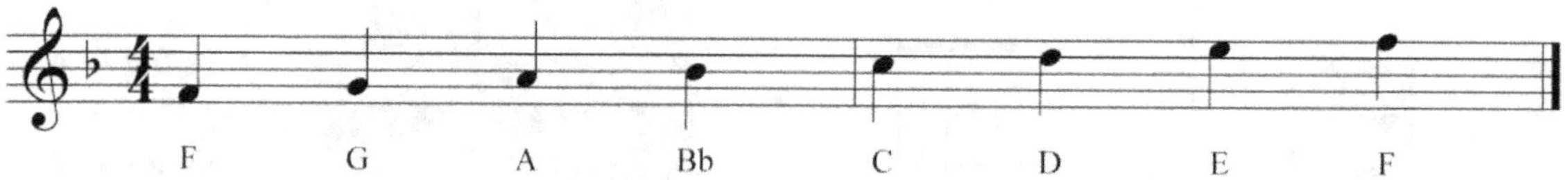

You can play B flat on the third string at the third fret with your third finger.

Exercise 1

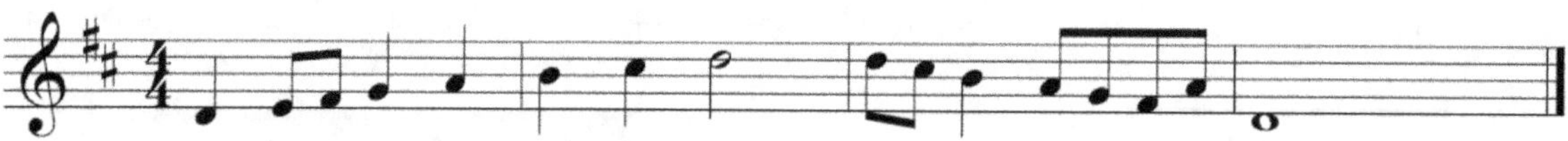

Exercise 2

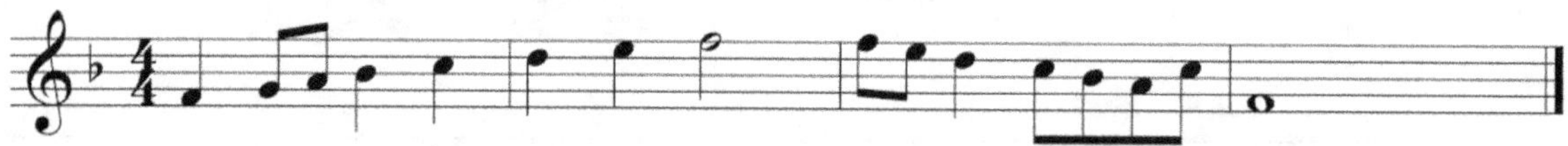

Remember that the accidentals in the key signature predefine the notes used for each scale, and this applies to all octaves.

Reading on the Top 4 Strings

Oh, Susanna

Clementine

Swing

To play with a swing, or shuffle, feel, the eighth notes are played with a specific rhythm, such that the eighth notes on the upbeats are delayed slightly. This rhythm is found in several styles of music—common in jazz and blues. Listen to the accompaniment MP3 collection to hear the swing feel of *Clementine*.

My Bonnie Lies Over The Ocean

Lesson Three

5th String or Open A

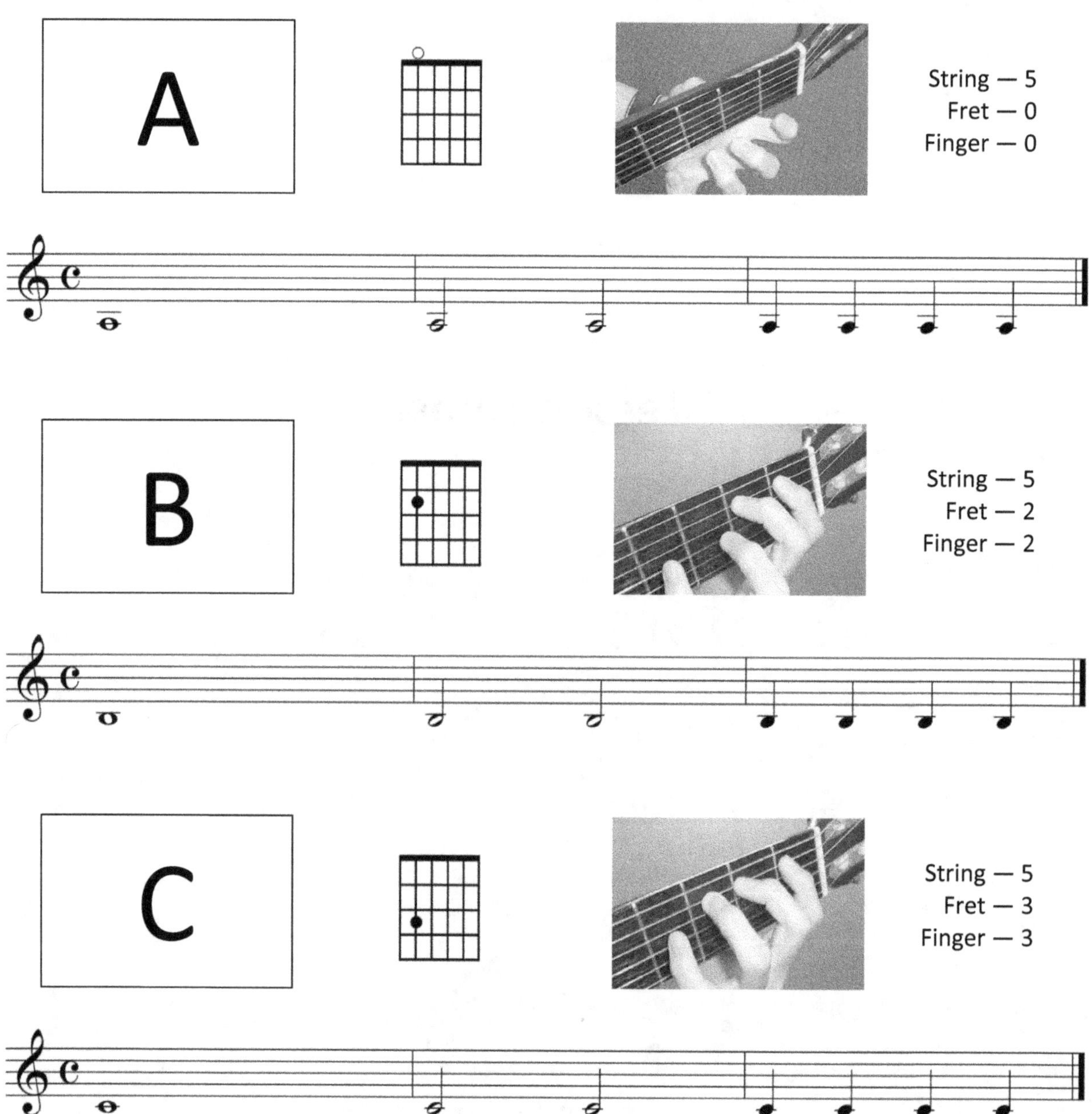

Remember to think about the names of the notes, where they're placed on the staff, where to play them on the fretboard, and which finger to use.

The C Major and B♭ Major Scales

C Major Scale

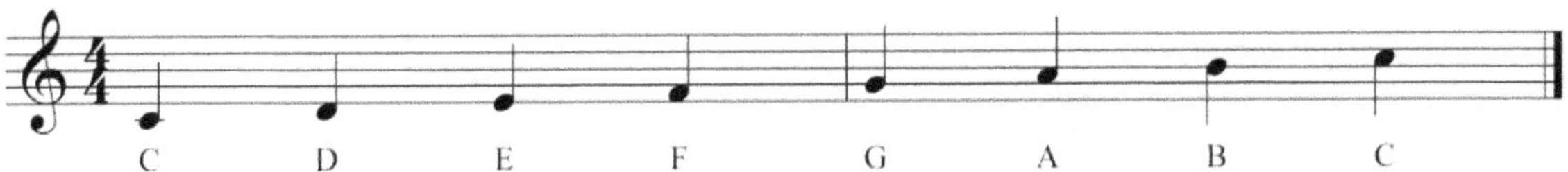

Notice that the key of C has no sharps or flats.

B♭ Major Scale

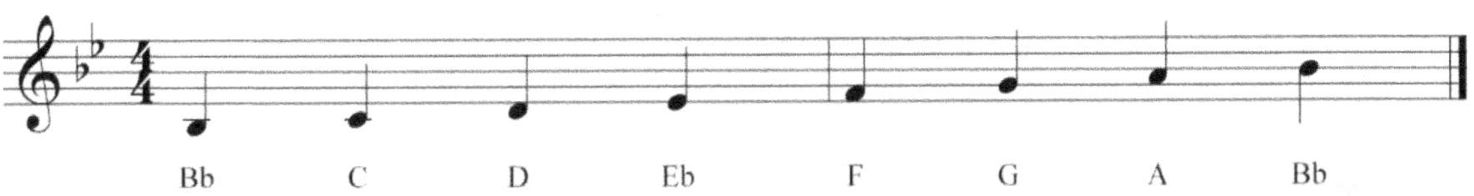

You can play B flat on the fifth string at the first fret with your first finger. You can play E flat on the fourth string at the first fret with your first finger.

Exercise 1

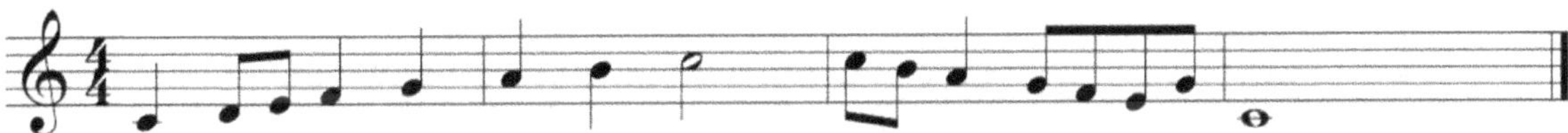

Exercise 2

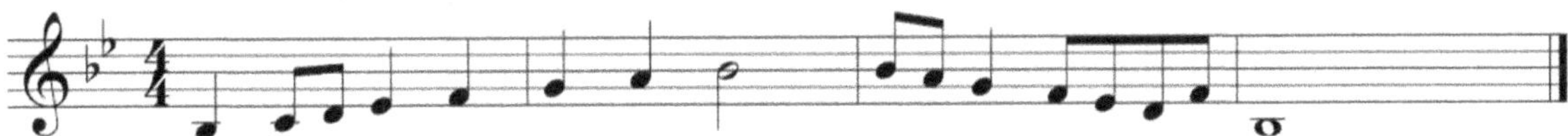

Exercises 1 and 2 have the same melody, but they're in different keys.

Reading on the Top 5 Strings

Itsy, Bitsy, Spider

Swing

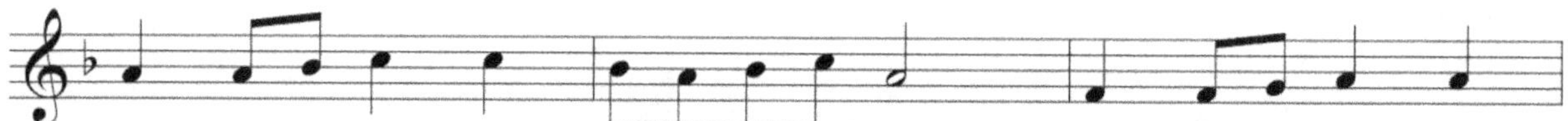

See Saw

The first and second endings are not played together. In *See Saw*, after completing the first ending, you follow the repeat sign to the beginning of the song and then, after the second time through, you skip the first ending and play the second ending instead.

Greensleeves

You can play C sharp on the fifth string at the fourth fret with your fourth finger.

Lesson Four

6th String or Open E

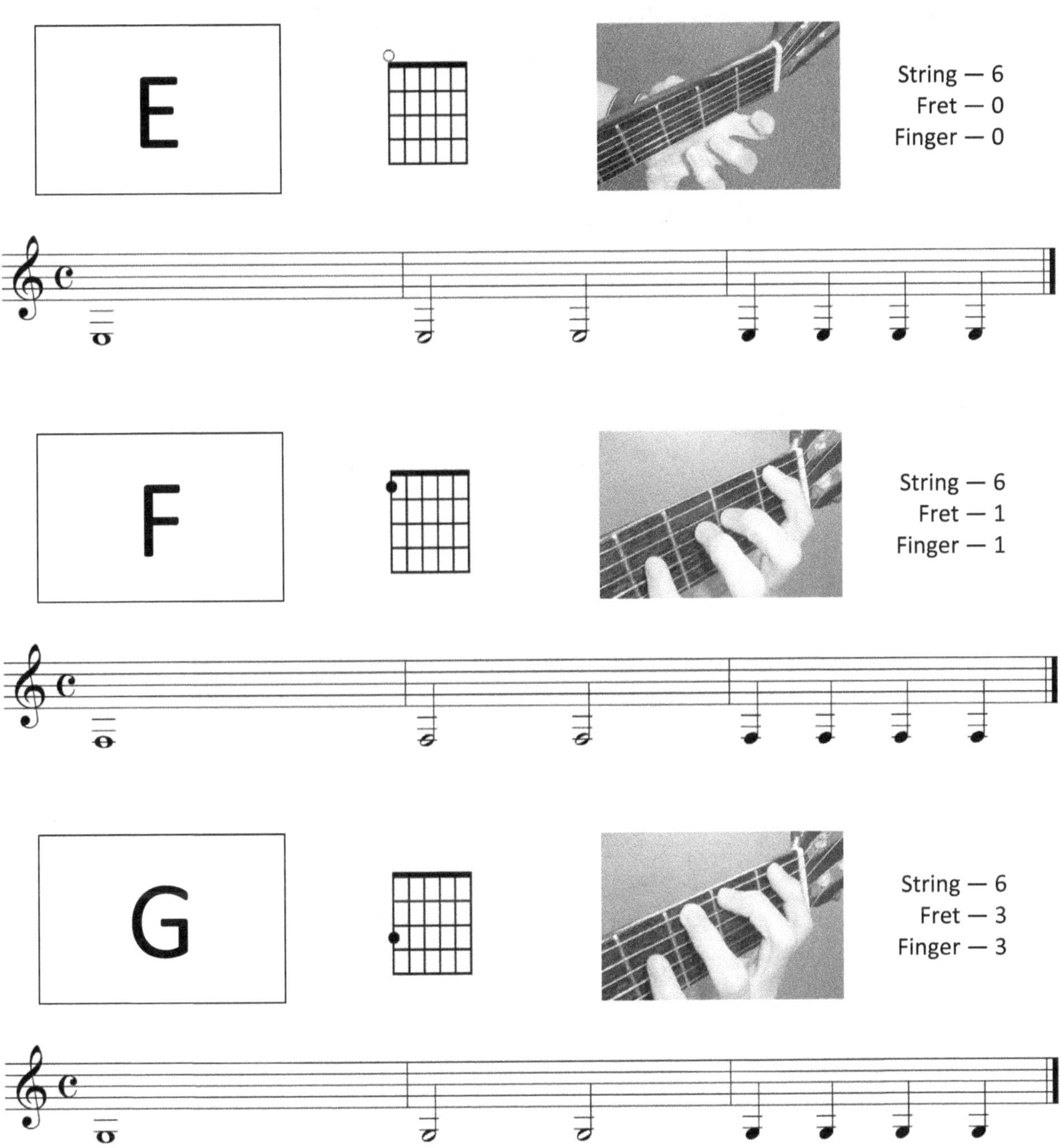

The sixth string open and the first string open are both called E, but they're two octaves apart. The difference can be seen on the staff as well as heard. You can now play three octaves of E, F, and G.

Exercise 1

Exercise 2

Bass Ickly

Swing

The natural accidental in *Bass Ickly* cancels the B flat for the duration of the measure.

Reading and Playing Full Chords

Now that you know all six strings in the open position, you can read and play open full chords. The G, G7, and C chords you learned in level one use the top three strings only, but now you can involve all strings.

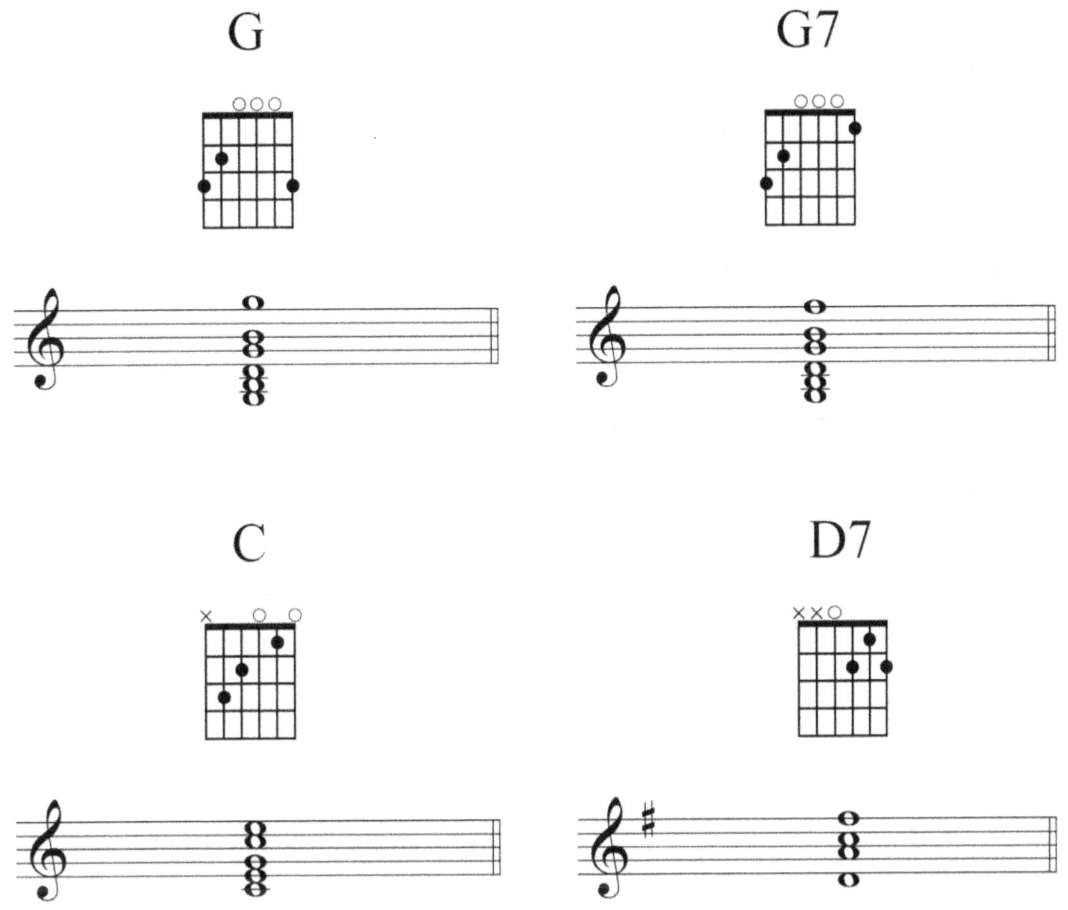

The "X" symbol above the nut specifies strings that are not used in the chord. This means that no sound should come from these strings.

Do Your Ears Hang Low?

Melodies 1 and 2 are the same melody, but an octave apart.

Lesson Five

Primary Chords

There are three primary chords, which create three different colours of harmony. Most songs can be played—if not precisely, at least passably—by using only primary chords.

When identifying a note's position in a key, we use Roman numerals, and the term "degree" is often used with these numbers. Different chords are built when starting from each of the seven degrees in a key.

Primary chords are built from the first degree (Tonic), the fourth degree (Subdominant), and the fifth degree (Dominant). Therefore, the three primary chords are the I chord, the IV chord, and the V chord.

Key	Accidentals in Key Signature	I	ii	iii	IV	V	vi	vii
C	0	C	D	E	F	G	A	B
G	1 sharp	G	A	B	C	D	E	F$^\sharp$
D	2 sharps	D	E	F$^\sharp$	G	A	B	C$^\sharp$
A	3 sharps	A	B	C$^\sharp$	D	E	F$^\sharp$	G$^\sharp$
E	4 sharps	E	F$^\sharp$	G$^\sharp$	A	B	C$^\sharp$	D$^\sharp$
B	5 sharps	B	C$^\sharp$	D$^\sharp$	E	F$^\sharp$	G$^\sharp$	A$^\sharp$
F$^\sharp$	6 sharps	F$^\sharp$	G$^\sharp$	A$^\sharp$	B	C$^\sharp$	D$^\sharp$	E$^\sharp$
C$^\sharp$	7 sharps	C$^\sharp$	D$^\sharp$	E$^\sharp$	F$^\sharp$	G$^\sharp$	A$^\sharp$	B$^\sharp$
F	1 flat	F	G	A	B$^\flat$	C	D	E
B$^\flat$	2 flats	B$^\flat$	C	D	E$^\flat$	F	G	A
E$^\flat$	3 flats	E$^\flat$	F	G	A$^\flat$	B$^\flat$	C	D
A$^\flat$	4 flats	A$^\flat$	B$^\flat$	C	D$^\flat$	E$^\flat$	F	G
D$^\flat$	5 flats	D$^\flat$	E$^\flat$	F	G$^\flat$	A$^\flat$	B$^\flat$	C
G$^\flat$	6 flats	G$^\flat$	A$^\flat$	B$^\flat$	C$^\flat$	D$^\flat$	E$^\flat$	F
C$^\flat$	7 flats	C$^\flat$	D$^\flat$	E$^\flat$	F$^\flat$	G$^\flat$	A$^\flat$	B$^\flat$

The V and V7 (*Dominant Seventh*) chords both function as chords built from the fifth degree.

Exercise 1

Name the key and its primary chords for each key signature.

a) Key of _____
I _____
IV _____
V _____

b) Key of _____
I _____
IV _____
V _____

c) Key of _____
I _____
IV _____
V _____

Exercise 2

Try to figure out the missing chords in *When the Saints Go Marching In*.

First, determine the key that you're playing in and name the I, IV, and V chords. At each "?" above the melody, a chord change occurs. You're only using three different chords in this song, so you only have two possible chords to try at each chord change. Listen to the melody with each chord you try, and using your ear, decide which chord sounds right. Fill in the missing chords to complete the song.

When The Saints Go Marching In

Lesson Six

Name These Melodies

1)

2)

3)

4)

If there are melodies here that you don't recognize, try playing them for your friends and family. Ask them if they can name these songs for you.

5)

6)

With these examples, you're reading and playing the music first and then trying to recognize the songs. The opposite of this is called lifting music, which is when you listen to a song first and then figure out how to play and write the music. The key of a song is one of the first things you need to determine when lifting music. By becoming familiar with the sharps or flats used in each key signature, you will be able to quickly recognize the key of any song that you're lifting.

Figure Out the Missing Notes

In the song below, *London Bridge Is Falling Down*, every "down" is missing a note on the staff. There are four notes missing and all are half notes. Try to figure out the pitch for each of these notes and then fill in these missing notes on the staff to complete the melody.

London Bridge Is Falling Down

In the song below, *Old MacDonald Had a Farm*, two measures are left empty. All missing notes are the same pitch. Figure out this pitch so that you know the name of the missing notes and then test your rhythm reading and writing skills by filling in the correct note values to complete the melody.

Old MacDonald Had A Farm

When you think you have figured out all the missing notes, play the song from beginning to end to hear if it sounds correct.

Lesson Seven

Classical Music

Classical Guitar Playing

Typically, playing the classical guitar involves holding the guitar a particular way, picking the strings with your thumb and fingers (fingerstyle), and reading the music precisely as written (no ad-libbing). It's a disciplined style that can be learned with regimented practice on the guitar and with study of this genre.

The song below, *Minuet in G*, is an example of music from this genre. A minuet is a musical form of a dance in moderate triple metre. Minuets were introduced into many operas and ballets and remained the most popular dance among the European aristocracy until the late 18th century.

Minuet In G

Johann Sebastian Bach

You can play this minuet with a pick because this simplified arrangement includes only the melody. If you choose to study classical guitar playing, you will learn how to play full arrangements using proper fingerstyle practices. This is just the first section of *Minuet in G*.

Country Music

Hammer-ons and Pull-offs

You play hammer-ons by picking a note and then hammering a finger onto the same string, while it's still vibrating, causing the pitch to change to a higher note without picking the string a second time.

You play pull-offs by playing a fretted note and then pulling off your finger, while the string is still vibrating, causing the pitch to change to a lower note.

Country Guitar Playing

There are many different guitar sounds in country music. One example can be created by using hammer-ons and pull-offs. The song below, *Country Sound*, illustrates this technique.

Country Sound

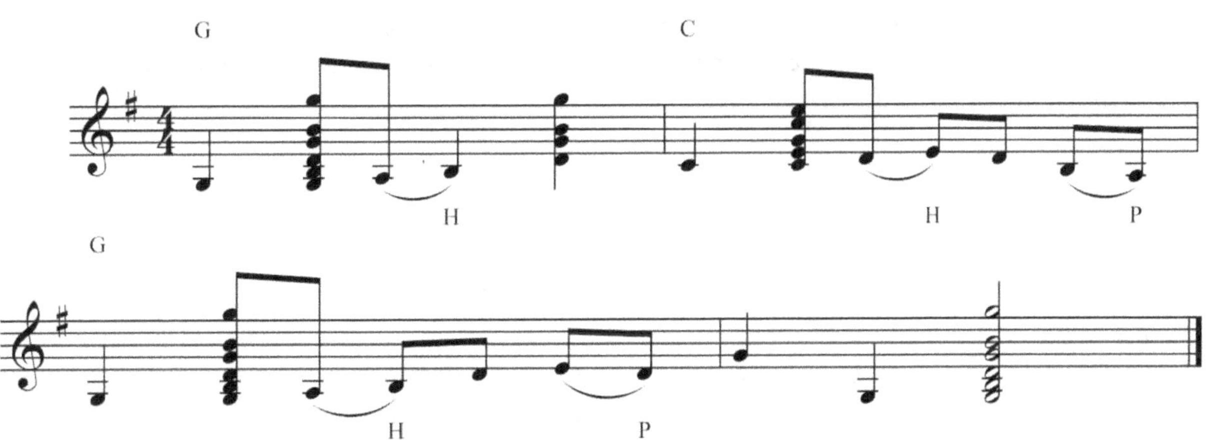

Hammer-ons and pull-offs are not restricted to country music; this technique is applied in many styles.

Jazz Music

Turnaround Progressions

In a turnaround progression, each time you reach the end of the progression, you turn around and start again from the beginning. This can repeat a specified number of times or as many times as players wish.

Chord Melodies

A chord melody is, as it sounds, a style of playing chords (harmony) and melody at the same time.

Jazz Guitar Playing

To play jazz guitar, you should learn about the rhythms and harmonies used in jazz music. You have learned about the swing feel and syncopation, which are both commonly used in jazz rhythms.

The song below, *Jazz Turnaround*, is a chord melody with a swing feel, and it introduces you to new harmonies. A triad is a basic chord made up of three notes. More notes (extensions) can be added to these triads to build up harmonies, changing the colours. These chords are so popular in jazz music that they're commonly referred to as jazz chords.

Jazz Turnaround (the I, vi, ii, V progression)

Typically, not every note from every chord gets played in chord melodies; however, chord names are often provided for reference.

Blues Music

Double-stop Riffs

Riffs are short, repeated phrases, and double stopping means to play two notes at the same time.

While playing through the chord changes of a blues progression, the rhythm players commonly play double-stop riffs. These riffs can be played with straight eighths or with a shuffle feel, which is similar to a swing feel.

In the song *Blues Riff*, the notes being played throughout the double-stop riff come from the chords written above the staff. You should try creating your own riffs, based on this example, to get a better feel for this style of playing.

Lesson Eight

Overview

Looking Back

You should be able to open this book to any page, count yourself in, and start playing any song or exercise without stopping. Making the odd mistake is fine, as long as you don't get stuck and stop playing in the middle of a song. If you can do this, you are ready to proceed to further levels.

Try playing several, if not all, of the songs and exercises in this book again, and test yourself to see if you are ready to proceed to further levels.

Looking Forward

At this point in your progress, you may favour particular areas of study. You are encouraged to continue your studies by following your interests. For example, you may be interested in focusing on a particular style of music. You may prefer melody playing, rhythm playing, or chord-melody playing. Now that you've learned the fundamentals, with all the good habits in place, you should continue studying however you wish, with classes, private instructions, or independently.

In *Strings Connected Workbook Just Chords*, you could focus on chord playing, if you wish. Lessons include strumming techniques, rhythm and style, chord structures, chord repertoire, common progressions, alternate bass, bass runs, fingerstyle playing, and other general musicianship skills.

Certificate of Completion

Certificate of Completion

This certifies that

____

has successfully completed the

Strings Connected Workbook Level Two

____
Date

____
Witness

www.ingramcontent.com/pod-product-compliance
Lightning Source LLC
Chambersburg PA
CBHW080315030726
47593CB00009B/2754